Poems of Salvation
with Illustrations & Photographs
by Thomas Henley Cayne

Poems of Salvation with Illustrations & Photographs by Thomas Henley Cayne © 2014 T.H. Cayne. All Rights Reserved.

Published and Printed in the USA by Shoe Music Press.
[*www.shoemusicpress.com*](www.shoemusicpress.com)

**Poems of Salvation
with Illustrations & Photographs
by Thomas Henley Cayne**

Poems:

The Long March 1

I release myself upon you 3

The comic distant ladder 4

The miracle within 6

Lazarus is waiting for the liquor to kick in 10

D—K (1-9) 13

D—K (2) - S.a.s.h.a (1-4) 17

Lack 20

The valley ahead (A question) 23

Bridged 24

Product of Truth (A tale of eight poems) 27

Faust 30

Air 33

Hyacinth and solitary bee 34

His, Manifesto 37

Oh, this insolent noise 38

Can You See Her? (At the bridge, every
single day to be beyond) 40

PATH 43

Illustrations:

The Legacy	facing page 1
The rule of war	2
Prune?	5
NEGATIVE OF ME	7
Portrait of a dead lady	8-9
Cup#3	11
Faceless girl (in stockings)	12
Girl in jeans	15
Sasha, waiting	16
Sasha, lying on sofa	18
Study of a girl	18-19
NRS series	21
Face of Elation	22
IMG_Dark	25
Iscariot 1	26
Iscariot 3	29
Cage	31
U-Dawn 1	32
U-Dawn 2	35
Photo 11	36-37
Iscariot 2	39

Contemplate 41

U-Dawn 3 42

Acknowledgements

The comic distant ladder appeared in Penny Ante Feud 10

Lazarus is waiting for the liquor to kick in appeared in Horror, Sleaze, Trash

D—K appeared in Sister Ignition

D—K (2) S.a.s.h.a. appeared in Sister Ignition

Can You See Her? (At the bridge, every single day to be beyond) appeared in Every day poets

About the model: the model featured in "Girl in jeans," "Sasha, lying on sofa," "Sasha, waiting" and "The rule of war" is *SX* (Alexandra "Sasha" Xiphias), whose dedication and inspiration is gratefully acknowledged.

Poems of Salvation
with Illustrations & Photographs
by Thomas Henley Cayne

To the month of May

The Legacy

The Long March

You feel the irony of faith. And intensely enjoy its cruelty.
You can't stop moving. Watching that rain. Solitary. Drops.

You think about (salvation).
Wait. Settle things.

Hungry. And. (Ready to fill the gap?)
OH — Refined.

As far as the fields of purslane stretch,
it comes to us —

(the sad porcelain clown shattered into a violent dream,
and his friend the broken limelight;
his nose bleeds vinegar;
a marble is heading for the filthy carpet floor;
one good eye still tries to grab a hold of this misery of a life;
his trousers seem to be owned by a baby with loving parents;
and above all, he tries to smile he tries to smile HE TRIES;
"where is this music coming from?";
"what about the feeling in my legs?";
"why don't you kiss me and take me with you, love?" — because
this is not the game;
the orange curls still on the head attached by sour glue;
semen — the white semen — his semen;
then the cleaning ladies begin to weep the floor;
and they clean it — they DO;
and he is gone)

that you are pursuing the long march.

And OH. (Once again.)
Refined.

The rule of war

I release myself upon you

I.
The long walk through the fields of clover
in that last summer,
the hiding shed to watch the birds.

When we arrived, I slowly forced you
on your knees, my beak into your mouth.
And managed to undo the knots
of the tiny laces which held your bathing suit together.

II.
Protesting when I threw your
clothes away, you kept going ahead,
now naked —

constant movements made you sink into the
soft sand of the birdhouse, your juicy lips touching
the ground —

III.
I see the old man approaching
through the peeping hole,
as I release myself upon you.

And then he tries to take you by surprise,
on your knees,
warm white lashes on your chin.

And you cry, moan, scream while you let him slide inside you,
looking at me with raging eyes —

You,
The kneeling Buddha of the semen.

The comic distant ladder

My pain sharpens the words
that you spread, in which you believe so
hard now.

Climbing far above me,
you try to kick off the rungs
so as to force me to the floor of the stair house.

Where you let me sleep every night
without sleep every night —
without sleep.

And I guess that is where I should have been.
Regretting the times when I still did matter.

For the flight — it starts below.

Not at the top of your comic
distant ladder.

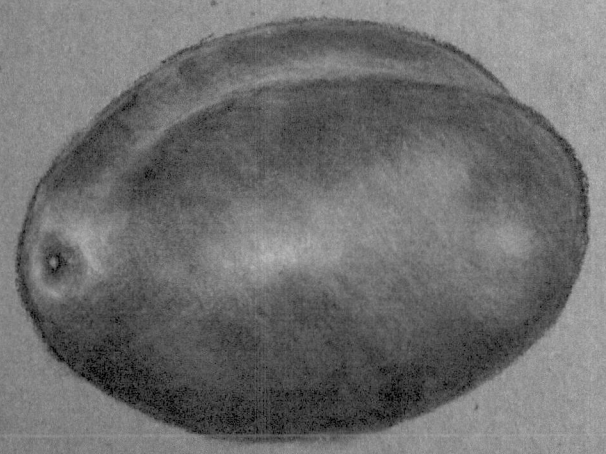

Prune?

The miracle within

Drives its tiny dust
through tiny cracks of doubt.

It has a smell.

The lies that shape your (love)
are hidden in my decayed flesh

and lit the blue
and kill the eyes.

Its sharpest force:

the dead man cries.

Portrait of a dead lady

Lazarus is waiting for the liquor to kick in

(And so we sing:)

Warns for the end,
claims he killed (love) —
a kind and teethless grin.

Thirty-some years old.
A white man's beard.
(HE HEARS THE COWBELLS CRYING?)

Carves shapes on knees
with rusty shards.
(HIS PRUNY WIFE LIES DYING.)

Ignored, not-listened-to,
beaten, tortured, laughed-at,
forgotten, stinking,
exhausted-white-trash-self-acclaimed-preacher-fucked up
LUNATIC.

Writes down cardboard signs —

Though in contrast to the other man.

He is NOT denying.

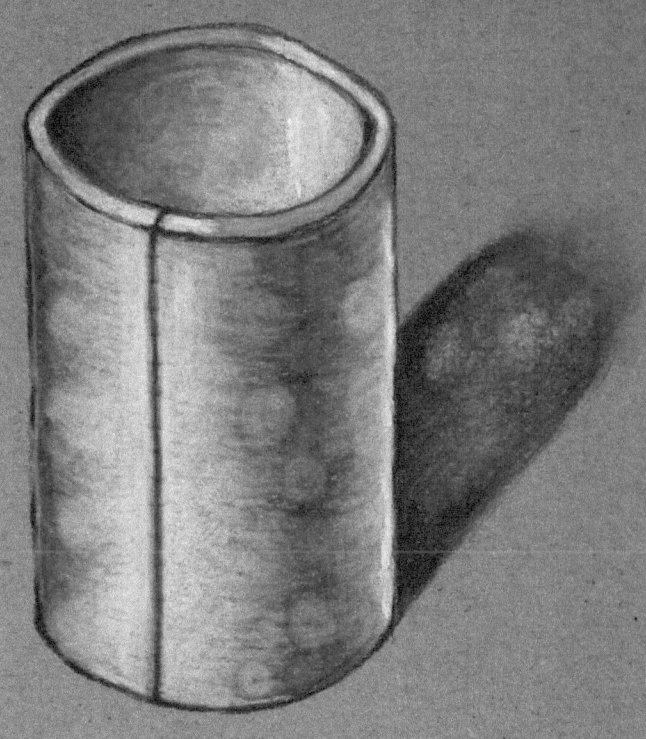

Cup#3

Faceless girl (in stockings)

D—K

1. We walk through rainy streets
and watch the prostitutes,
wondering what they do behind the curtains.

2. We see the two black girls in white undies
knocking on windows
and willing for hard cash.

3. We go inside and drink more beer and smell the sweet distant
salty flavor of used condoms, mixed with drops of heavy
perfume. We don't know what we're doing there, but there is no
way back it seems, and the horny distress
is so confusing. We get undressed.

4. One of them slowly erects my penis
with her pink tongue as the other much younger
girl kisses your belly and thighs with my fingers inside her.
And the all too distant music leads us further in the whore hole
of the night.

5. I watch them take you while you scream, and I make drawings.
I come inside all of you till it hurts. And then
you go down on me in pain. And when you are exhausted, we
pay them more to fuck each other, and they do it.

6. But this is fine because everything is deeply hidden in the
inside. And they like the cum, and the pussy juice.
And they are so nice, and taste so sweet and filthy.

7. And so did you.

(Continued on page 14)

(Continued from page 13)

8. But I liked the darkness.

9. And I miss the sight —
Not of winning.
And certainly not of you.
But still, I might.

Sasha, waiting

D—K (2) - S. a. s. h. a.

1. You want to dress up, just like her. This image of the woman that you are, the whore that was always there, of which you are ashamed. But he tells you to come out, in night, in dark, in silent semen.

2. In the pub, the harbor, the city, the alcohol, the smiles, the sweat. You are short-skirted. You are naked underneath. You are horny underneath.

You want the words. The photographs. You do not want to ask.

You want to be asked.

3. She sucks the ugly old men through the stinking glory hole of denial. She swallows the semen of the lies. The cum of man. The flies.

4. The door is open. She is exposed. She is fucked. In sex hotels. The creaking sounds of sticky beds and filthy drapes. But still she spreads. And turns her head — for Taste.

For she is asked.

Sasha, lying on sofa

Study of a girl

Lack

This pain is hard to bare.
Fainted on the marble floor, head struck, bloody taste, drums that BEAT, drops of sweat on walls, shit water that mixes with the white veins of the Rosso Levanto.
I do not move.
I haven't fainted in years.
I want to move.
I can't move.
My heart POUNDS through my lower body, right up to the shithole that makes this mess — the door is open.
A woman stares, with shame — I only see her see-through underwear, lips, shoes.
(What is she doing in my house.)
I try to scratch the floor, to make it bleed, to suck the light, to breathe.
Make drawings on the floor with my knees. Clean the door with toes.
(I cannot move my arms.)
I try to sing a cozy tune.
(Why do we try so hard?)
Something HITS me with a brick, and opens my head.
I wet myself. Urine flows.
I see the veins.

And it is good.

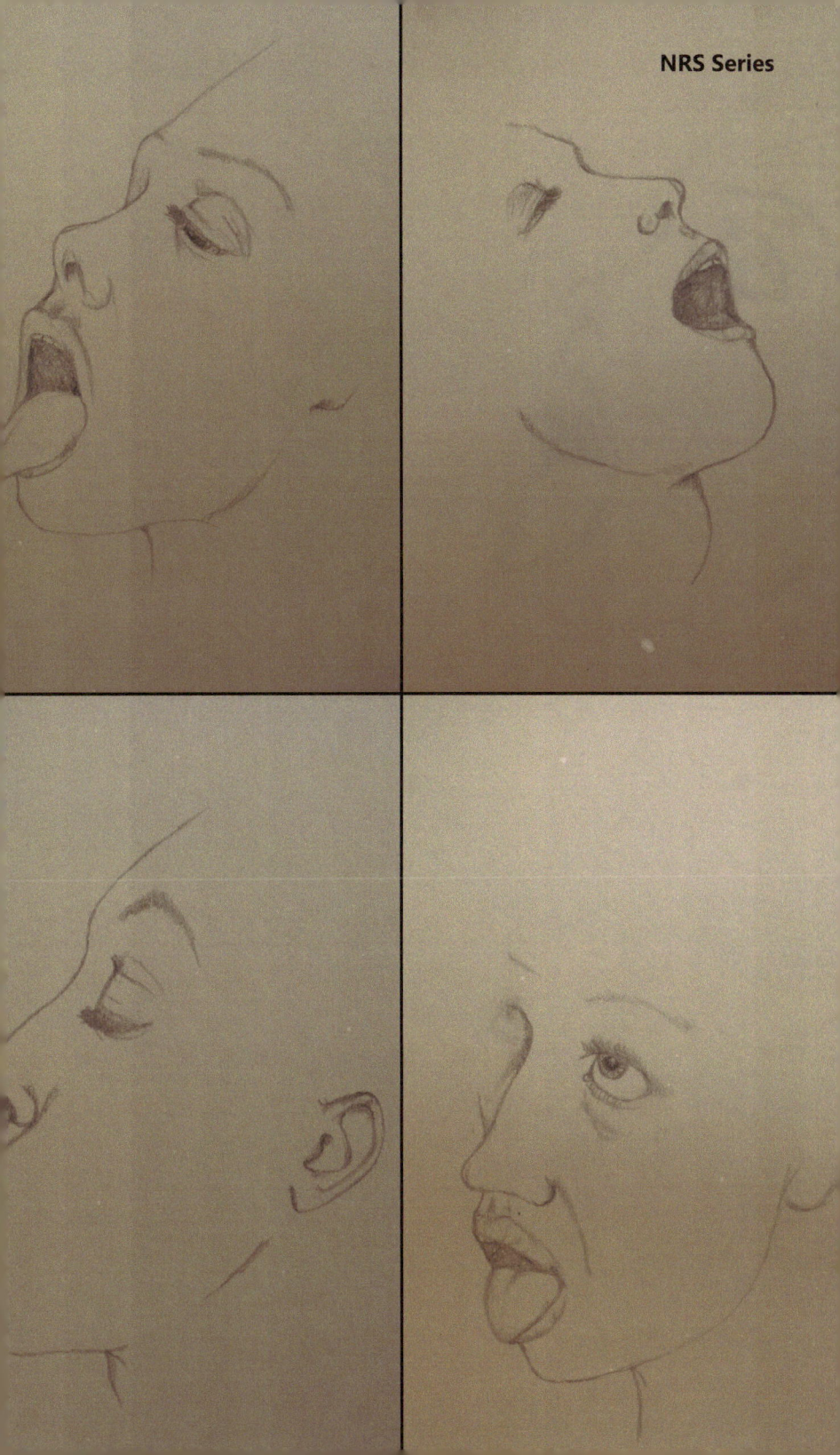

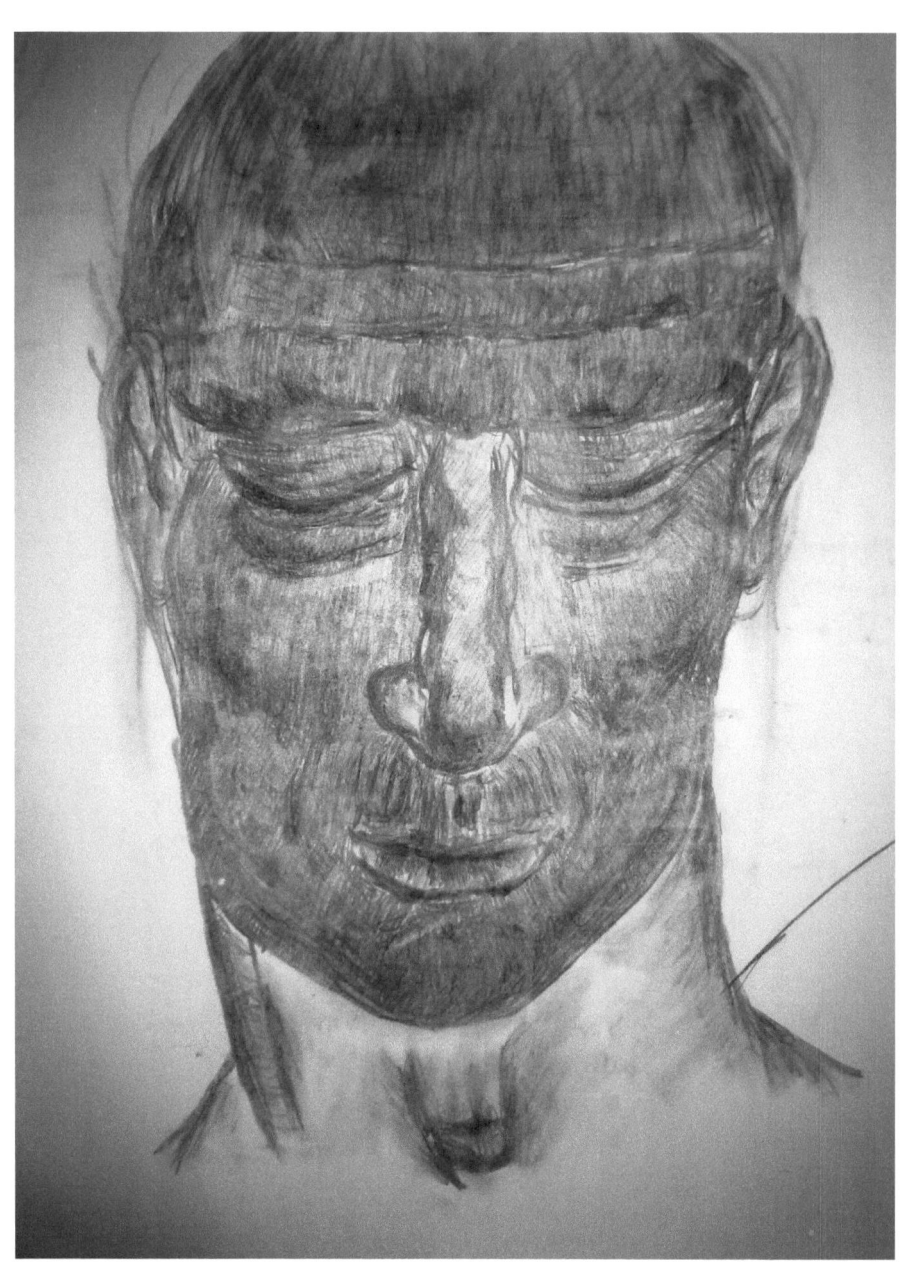

Face of Elation

The valley ahead (A question)

"How could this happen?
How could this be?

Why did (love) leave this broken body,
And leave it, to see —

The edge of (salvation);
The valley ahead;
The things that I did;
The words that she said.

Eyes of the blue,
Morbidly thinking:

It all comes to you."

Bridged

On the 18th of November
he starts seeing the stains.

Not knowing, not asking,
not showing — but something is projected
onto a shadow of rusty marks.

He tries to penetrate but cannot come
any closer —

words hit the wooden ceiling without an echo
anymore.

Then panics, cannot get rid of this image.
River of coral red drops which follows us, or them?

He is not clean, and carries the filth of secrets
of the pictures and the wigs, the girls which
stand aside.

And tries to wipe out that
deep in night,
dark woven times are right ahead.

No tufted titmouse makes a noise.

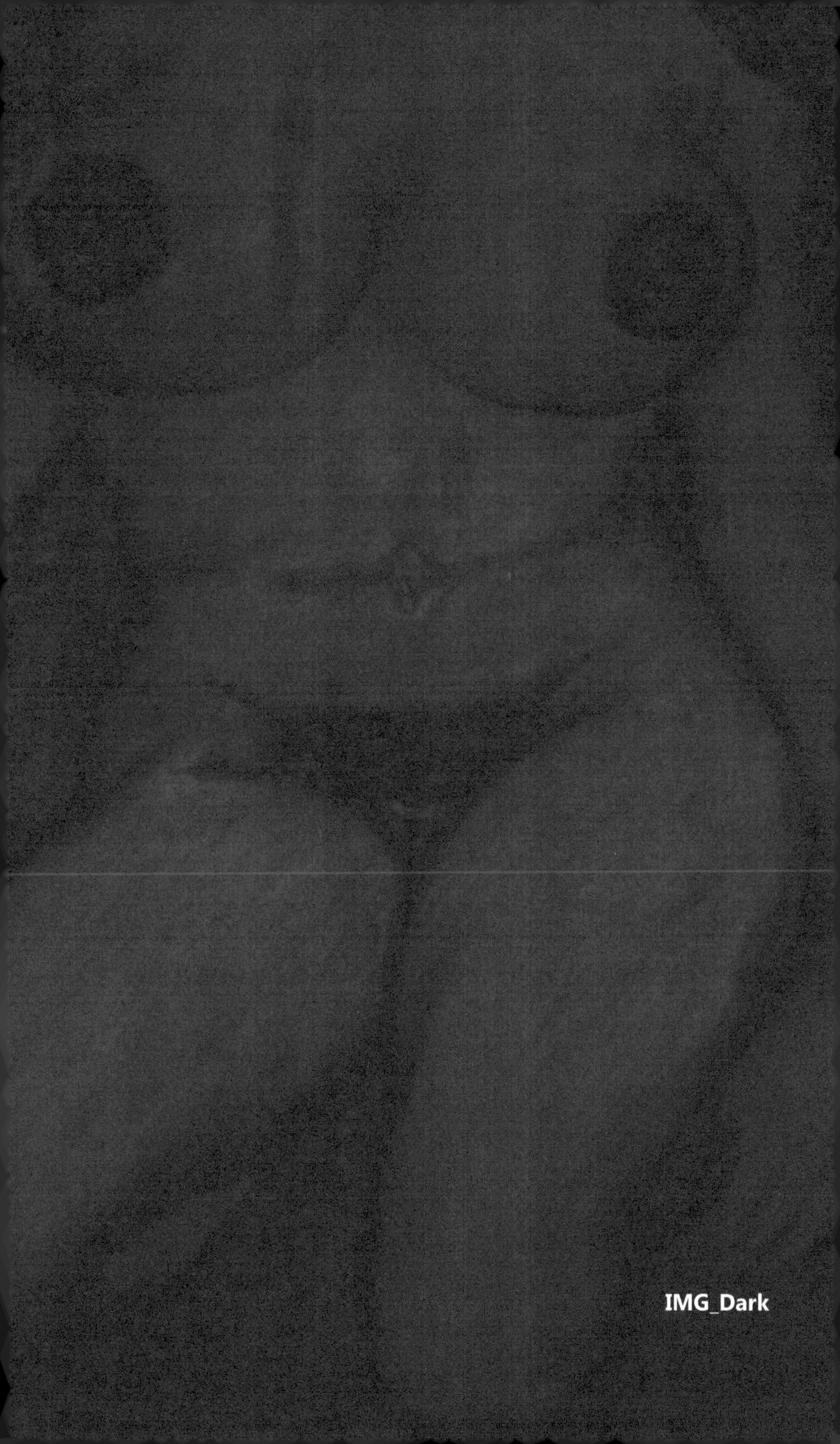
IMG_Dark

Iscariot 1

Product of Truth (A tale of eight poems)

1. He is the first to notice?

When the silent man cries,
the tears of his wife near the cross in the dirt,
because she knew he was going.

When she screamed:
"The goal of the path is the path."
"Not the goal."

That difference is what they did not see.
When the silent man cried,
and (love) turned its tired head —

He is born.

2. Many years later — he still hears the cries —
the voices keep turning —
his mind into lies.

And after a while, the migraine sets in,
he vomits and bleeds,
but still hears her voice.

3. As yet again later
the silent man cries,
he now wants the answer,
sleeps nights back to back,
the difference too heavy,
betraying his youth,
his head hurting bad.

(Continued on page 28)

(Continued from page 27)

4. The torment of knowing,
Through night upon night, that
He is the product.

5. Night upon night.
Upon night upon night.
Upon night.

6. And there is no father. And there is no mother.

7. And many years later he still hears the cries. The voices keep turning — his mind into lies.
He knows the (salvation).
For He is the choice.

8. And when she arrives, she is already too late.
For He is the product, and she is the bait.

Iscariot 3

Faust

Was he about to sell his soul (and for what) —
Did he want eternal wisdom, or at least for 24 years,
one for every hour at the rock-around-the-clock?
Have fallen females in his bed, juicy and perfumed,
just for his sake?
To forget an old love who had disappeared in the
end of light, not knowing her possible putrid pain
that he could have caused?

Or did he want compassion,
be the central force,
instead of being laughed at
despite his (obvious?) talent?

Hating the ticking in the empty room
(empty, even with him in it).

Listen to this little sound of nothing. (Squeak?)

Or did he wish for a single, honest
smile? —

from YOU.

Air

I am not sure why she was smiling,
but she was.

They were all dead — poses of torment and sighs
penetrated the field of clover, and
she just grinned. (I nearly vomited.)

As far as we could see.

I tried to push my hands through the grain light
where mere mortals could not reach.
I tried a lot.

Far away were the weeping giants.

I noticed toads that made a squeaky sound as they sat there
in oblivion by the hundreds.

I noticed a woman who was lying in the dirt, naked,
touching herself, screaming in silence. Red blushed
baby sweet.

I did not notice the pain in my left arm, which made the air
so heavy.

And made me rest a bit.

Hyacinth and solitary bee

Spot her as she lies down on the cold stone floor.

Try to reach the window to say "hello."
Smell the flower. Feel the stings.

The arms are heavy (so heavy).

Little robin hops through the grass and ignores.
(Its delicate chest reveals her beautiful taste.
Thorny eyes see right through me. And they whisper.)

And then the insects,
on the dark dunes,
with the heath.

And then the fleas.

(Underneath the humming are footsteps
coming from the kitchen door.)

I am guessing — am I guessing?
I am singing — do I sing?
I am lying — can I move?
I am bleeding — hard to breathe.

(That.)

(Something is inside.)

For more.

His, Manifesto

"Sucking up the energy of others — I will not be like THEM."
The light. (Inside?)
"Proceeding as I were — existing." Is. (The word?)
"Not hating. Not forgiving. Seeing — breathe." Reaching. (Up?)
"I will have to. I will carry (away)."
"On the dirt." Up. (To?)
"Butterflies will follow. And so will they. NOT to see."
"Them coming (all)." To. (?)
ME.

Oh, this insolent noise

Whispers of betrayal found their way
dancing on his shoulders
feasting in the dark room —
a taste of dead tortoise soup,
hint of a murder triandrus Daffodil.

He knew that this could happen
having seen the eyes in mirrors
but having not foreseen the madness
of the queen.

Her flesh, an open wound for ages,
had found a way to crawl,
and bite.

Now driven by cowardice of others,
not denying what is so clear, he
needs the blood so bad.

The bugs confuse him, the noise is strange.
He knows that it is there.

Clouds of green Hairstreak butterflies move by, and
confuse him even more. They are the color of dawn.

He kicks the flesh, hard. For they don't wait.

(They show the way.)

Can You See Her?
(At the bridge, every single day to be beyond)

Its spirit broke.

(Single spark —)

The other side, a glimpse of dream, some color. Green.

I do not plan to go back.

(Tiny snap — .)

Contemplate

PATH

He wanted to taste the salt from her eyes,
moved by the deep catatonic sleep she apparently was in.
She would never know. (Did she need to?)

Still feeling the throbbing pain in his neck, he touched the marks. The bloody
crusts seemed dry now —
The little moths so ready.

About the Author

Thomas Henley Cayne is a US painter and writer — he currently lives in Europe, alternating between Denmark and The Netherlands.

A prolific painter and writer since "the beginning of time," he started to publish his visual and written artwork only quite recently, has accepted poems and short stories in several languages, and accepted visual artwork in a host of art magazines.

Cayne eats, drinks, sleeps, paints and writes. But that is not all.

www.ingramcontent.com/pod-product-compliance
Lightning Source LLC
Chambersburg PA
CBHW041757040426
42446CB00005B/236